ARIANA GRANDE

Biography of a Self-Made Legend

Info Edge

Info Edge Publications

Info
Edge
Publications

CONTENTS

ARIANA GRANDE

EARLY LIFE

Ariana Grande-Butera was brought into the world on June 26, 1993, in Boca Raton, Florida. She is the girl of Joan Grande, the Brooklyn-conceived CEO of Hose-McCann Communications, a maker of interchanges and security gear, and Edward Butera, a visual depiction firm proprietor in Boca Raton. Grande is of Italian plunge and has depicted herself as an Italian American with Sicilian and Abruzzese roots. She has a more seasoned stepbrother, Frankie Grande, who is a performer and maker, and she has a cozy relationship with her maternal grandma, Marjorie Grande. Her family moved from New York to Florida before her introduction to the world, and her folks isolated when she was eight or nine years of age.

At the point when her folks were Florida Panthers season ticket holders, she was inadvertently hit on every wrist by deviant hockey pucks on two unique events in 1998, supporting minor injuries the twice. The subsequent event occurred during the Panthers' debut ordinary season game at National Car Rental Center on October 9, 1998, in which she was additionally the primary youngster to at any point ride a Zamboni in the spic and span field during the principal break, the consequence of her folks' $200 winning offered at a closeout. A photo of her on the Zamboni was included in the South Florida SunSentinel the following day. At age 8, she sang "The Star-Spangled Banner" at the Panthers' home game against the Chicago Blackhawks on January 16, 2002.

As a little youngster, Grande performed with the Fort Lauderdale Children's Theater, playing her first job as the title character in the melodic Annie. She additionally acted in their developments of The Wizard of Oz and Beauty and the Beast. At age eight, she performed at a karaoke relax on a voyage transport and with different ensembles like South Florida's Philharmonic, Florida Sunshine Pops, and Symphonic Orchestras. During this time, she went to the Pine Crest School and later North Broward Preparatory.

CAREER START

2008–2012

By age 13, Grande became genuine about seeking after a music vocation, in spite of the fact that she actually focused on theater. At the point when she initially showed up in Los Angeles, California to meet with her chiefs, she communicated a craving to record a R&B collection: "I resembled, 'I need to make a R&B collection,' They resembled 'Um, that is a helluva objective! Who will purchase a 14-year-old's R&B album?!'" In 2008, Grande was given a role as team promoter Charlotte in the Broadway melodic 13. At the point when she joined the melodic, Grande left North Broward Preparatory School, yet kept on being selected; the school sent her materials to review with mentors. She additionally sang different occasions at the New York City jazz club Birdland.

Grande was projected in the Nickelodeon TV program Victorious alongside 13 co-star Elizabeth

Gillies in 2009. In the sitcom, set at a performing expressions secondary school, she played the "delightfully dumb" Cat Valentine. She needed to color her hair red each and every week for the job, which seriously harmed her hair. The show debuted in March 2010 to the second-biggest crowd for a surprisingly realistic series in Nickelodeon, with 5.7 million watchers. The job impelled Grande to teenager symbol status, yet she was more keen on a music profession, saying that acting is "fun, however music has been above all else all of the time with me." Her personality was contrasted with "Brittany Murphy's presentation as the hapless Tai in Clueless" and portrayed as being "truly naive and handily influenced" yet "for the most part sweet". She likewise played Miriam in the melodic Cuba Libre, composed and created by American musician Desmond Child.

After the principal period of Victorious wrapped, Grande needed to zero in on her music vocation and started chipping away at her presentation collection in August 2010. To fortify her vocal reach, she started working with vocal mentor Eric Vetro. The subsequent season debuted in April 2011 to 6.2 million watchers, turning into the show's most elevated evaluated episode. In May 2011, Grande showed up in Greyson Chance's video for the melody "Unfriend You" from his collection Hold On until the Night (2011), depicting his ex. She showed up on the track "Surrender It" from the Victorious soundtrack in August 2011. While shooting Victorious, Grande made a few accounts of herself singing fronts of tunes by Adele, Whitney Houston, and Mariah Carey, and transferred them to YouTube. A companion of Monte Lipman, (CEO) of Republic Records, went over one of the recordings. Intrigued by her vocals, he sent the connections to Lipman, who marked her to a recording contract. Grande voiced the lead spot in the English name of the Spanish-language enlivened film Snowflake, the White Gorilla in November 2011. From 2011 to 2013, she voiced the pixie Princess Diaspro in the Nickelodeon restoration of Winx Club.

In December 2011, Grande delivered her first single, "Put Your Hearts Up", which was recorded for a potential youngster arranged pop collection that was rarely given. She later repudiated the track for its bubblegum pop sound, saying she cared very little about recording music of that sort. The tune was subsequently affirmed Gold by the Recording Industry Association of America (RIAA). On a subsequent soundtrack, Victorious 2.0, delivered on June 5, 2012, as a lengthy play, she provided vocals as a component of the show's cast for the tune "5 Fingaz to the Face". The third and last soundtrack, Victorious 3.0, was delivered on November 6, 2012, including Grande duetting with Victoria Justice in the melody "L.A. Boyz". A music video followed. In December 2012, Grande teamed up on the single form of "Famous Song", a two part harmony with British artist and musician Mika.

After four seasons, Victorious was not restored,

with the finale broadcasting in February 2013. Grande featured as Snow White in the emulate style melodic theater creation A Snow White Christmas with Charlene Tilton and Neil Patrick Harris at the Pasadena Playhouse. She played Amanda Benson in Swindle, a 2013 Nickelodeon film transformation of the kids' book of a similar name. In the mean time, Nickelodeon made Sam and Cat, an early and Victorious side project featuring Jennette McCurdy and Grande. Grande and McCurdy repeated their jobs as Cat Valentine and Sam Puckett on the amigo sitcom, which matched the characters as flat mates who structure an after-school minding. The pilot broadcasted on June 8, 2013, and the organization quickly got the show. The following month, Nickelodeon multiplied Sam and Cat's unique 20-episode request for season one, making it a 40-episode season. In spite of its achievement in the evaluations, the series was dropped after 35 episodes. The last episode circulated on July 17, 2014.

SLOW RISE

2013–2015

Grande recorded her presentation studio collection Yours Truly, initially named Daydreamin', north of three years. It was delivered on August 30, 2013, and appeared at number one on the US Billboard 200 collections outline, with 138,000 duplicates sold in its first week. Yours Truly additionally appeared in the best ten of every few different nations, including Australia, the UK, Ireland, and the Netherlands. Its lead single, "The Way", highlighting Pittsburgh rapper Mac Miller, appeared at number ten on the US Billboard Hot 100, ultimately cresting at number nine for a considerable length of time. Grande was subsequently sued by Minder Music for duplicating the line "What we must do here is return, back on schedule" from the 1972 tune "Ignoramus (Cave Man)" by The Jimmy Castor Bunch. The collection's subsequent single, "Child I", was delivered in July. Its third single, "In that general area", including Detroit rapper Big Sean, was delivered in August 2013. They individually crested at number 21 and 84 on the Billboard Hot 100.

Grande recorded the two part harmony "Nearly Is Never Enough" with Nathan Sykes of The Wanted, which was delivered as a special single in August 2013. She additionally joined Justin Bieber on his Believe Tour for three shows and started off her featuring smaller than expected visit, The Listening Sessions. The next month, Billboard magazine positioned Grande at number four on their rundown of "Music's Hottest Minors 2013", a yearly positioning of the most well known performers younger than 21. At the 2013 American Music Awards, she won the honor for New Artist of the Year. She delivered a four-melody Christmas EP, Christmas Kisses in December 2013. Grande got the Breakthrough Artist of the Year grant from the Music Business Association, perceiving her accomplishments all through 2013. By January 2014, Grande had started recording her second studio collection, with vocalist lyricist Ryan Tedder and record makers Benny Blanco and Max Martin. That very month, she acquired the Favorite Breakout Artist grant at the People's Choice Awards 2014. In March 2014, Grande sang at the White House show, "Ladies of Soul: In Performance at the White House". The next month, President Barack Obama and First Lady Michelle Obama welcomed Grande again to perform at the White House for the Easter Egg Roll occasion.

Grande delivered her second studio collection My Everything on August 25, 2014, and appeared on the Billboard 200. Its lead single "Issue" highlights Australian rapper Iggy Azalea and debuted at the 2014 Radio Disney Music Awards on April 26, 2014. The melody appeared at number three (ultimately moving to number two) on the Billboard Hot 100, and appeared at number one on the UK Singles Chart, turning into Grande's first number-one single in the United Kingdom. The collection's subsequent single, "Break Free", highlighting German artist and maker Zedd, topped at number four in the United States. She played out the melody at the launch of the 2014 MTV Video Music Awards and won Best Pop Video for "Issue". Grande and Nicki Minaj gave visitor vocals on "Bang", the lead single from Jessie J's collection Sweet Talker, which crested at number one in the UK and arrived at number three in the US. With the singles "Issue", "Break Free", and "Bang", Grande joined Adele as the main female craftsman with three top ten singles at the same time on the Billboard Hot 100 as a lead craftsman.

Grande was the melodic entertainer on Saturday Night Live, with Chris Pratt as the host on September 27, 2014. That very month, the third single from My Everything, "Love Me Harder", highlighting Canadian recording craftsman The Weeknd, was delivered and topped at number seven in the United States. The melody turned into her fourth top-ten single of 2014, the most by any craftsman that year. In November 2014, Grande was included in Major Lazer's melody "All My Love" from the soundtrack collection for the film The Hunger Games: Mockingjay - Part 1 (2014). That very month, Grande delivered a Christmas tune named "Santa Clause Tell Me" as a solitary from the reissue of her first Christmas EP, Christmas Kisses (2014). She later set the fifth and the last single free from My Everything, "One final Time", which topped at number 13 in the US.

In February 2015, Grande set out on her first overall show visit, The Honeymoon Tour, to additionally advance My Everything, with shows in North America, Europe, Asia, and South America. Grande was highlighted on Cashmere Cat's tune "Venerate", which was delivered in March 2015. In the spring, she marked an elite distributing contract with the Universal Music Publishing Group, covering her whole music list. Grande likewise recorded an episode for the Fox Broadcasting Company unscripted television series Knock Live (2015), yet the show was dropped before her episode circulated. She likewise visitor featured on a few episodes of the Fox parody frightfulness TV series Scream Queens as Sonya Herrmann/Chanel#2 from September to November 2015. She recorded the two part harmony "E Più Ti Penso" with Italian recording craftsman Andrea Bocelli, which was delivered in October 2015 as the lead single from Bocelli's collection Cinema (2015), and covered the tune "Zero to Hero", initially from the enlivened film Hercules (1997), for the aggregation collection We Love Disney (2015). Grande additionally delivered her second Christmas EP, Christmas and Chill in December 2015.

DANGEROUS WOMAN

2015–2017

Grande started recording melodies for her third studio collection, Dangerous Woman, initially named Moonlight, in 2015. In October of that year, she delivered the single "Concentration", at first planned as the lead single from the collection; the tune appeared at number seven on the Billboard Hot 100. The following month American vocalist Who Is Fancy delivered the single "Young men Like You", which includes her and Meghan Trainor. She was highlighted in the remix adaptation of "Again and again", a tune by English vocalist Nathan Sykes' introduction studio solo collection Unfinished Business, which was delivered in January 2016. Grande showed up in the satire film Zoolander 2 featuring Ben Stiller and Owen Wilson. In March 2016, Grande delivered "Hazardous Woman" as the lead single from the retitled collection of a similar name. The single appeared at number ten on the Billboard Hot 100, turning into the main craftsman to have the lead single from every one of her initial three collections debut in the best ten. That very month, Grande showed up as host and melodic visitor of Saturday Night Live, where she performed "Hazardous Woman" and appeared in the limited time single "Be Alright", which diagrammed at number 43 on the Billboard Hot 100. Grande collected positive surveys for her appearance on the show, including acclaim for her impressions of different vocalists, some of which she had done on The Tonight Show. Grande won an internet casting ballot survey on Entertainment Weekly as the "best host of the period". In May 2016, Grande showed up on The Voice season 10 finale, playing out the second single from the collection, "Into You", which topped at number 13 in the United States, and duetted with Christina Aguilera on "Hazardous Woman".

Grande delivered Dangerous Woman on May 20, 2016, and appeared at number two on the Billboard 200. It likewise appeared at number two in Japan, and at number one of every few different business sectors, including Australia, the Netherlands, Ireland, Italy, New Zealand, and the UK. Mark Savage, composing for BBC News, referred to the collection as "an experienced, certain record". At the Summertime Ball at London's Wembley Stadium in

June, Grande performed three melodies from the collection as a component of her set. In August, Grande let a third single out of the collection, "Side to Side", highlighting rapper Nicki Minaj, her eighth top ten section on the Hot 100, which topped at number four on that outline. Perilous Woman was assigned for Grammy Award for Best Pop Vocal Album and the title track for Best Pop Solo Performance.

In August 2016, Grande played out a recognition for the late Whitney Houston on the season finale of the ABC TV series Greatest Hits and featured the premiere night of the second yearly Billboard Hot 100 Music Festival, playing out an almost extended arrangement of her tunes. Besides music, Grande shot a business for T-Mobile that debuted in October 2016 and played Penny Pingleton in the NBC transmission Hairspray Live!, which was broadcast in December 2016. That very month, Grande and Stevie Wonder showed up on the season finale of the US contest TV series The Voice, playing out their coordinated effort "Confidence" from the soundtrack of the 2016 enlivened film Sing. "Confidence" was selected for Best Original Song at the 74th Golden Globe Awards. Toward the year's end, Grande partook in the Jingle Ball Tour 2016. Grande recorded the title track of the soundtrack for 2017 true to life revamp of Disney's 1991 enlivened film Beauty and the Beast. The recording was delivered as a two-part harmony with American artist John Legend in February 2017. That very month, Grande left on her third show visit, the Dangerous Woman Tour, to advance the connected collection. On April 27, 2017, Norwegian DJ Cashmere Cat delivered the fifth melody "Quit" from his introduction collection 9 highlighting Grande.

On May 22, 2017, her show at Manchester Arena was the objective of self-destruction bombarding a shrapnel-loaded custom-made bomb exploded by an Islamic fanatic as individuals were leaving the field. The Manchester Arena bombarding caused 22 passings and harmed hundreds more. Grande suspended the rest of the visit and held a broadcast benefit show, One Love Manchester, on June 4, assisting with raising $23 million to help the besieging's casualties and impacted families. The show highlighted exhibitions from Grande, just as Liam Gallagher, Robbie Williams, Justin Bieber, Katy Perry, Miley Cyrus, and different craftsmen. To perceive her endeavors, the Manchester City Council named Grande the primary privileged resident of Manchester. The visit continued on June 7 in Paris and finished in September 2017. In August 2017, Grande showed up in an Apple Music Carpool Karaoke episode, singing melodic theater tunes with American performer Seth MacFarlane. In December 2017, Billboard magazine named her "Female Artist of the Year".

SWEETENER AND THANK U, NEXT

2018–2019

G rande started chipping away at melodies for her fourth studio collection, Sweetener, with Pharrell Williams in 2016, however, "the occasions in Manchester gave a hard reset to the venture's assumptions". Grande delivered "No Tears Left to Cry" as the lead single from Sweetener in April 2018, with the tune appearing at number three on the Billboard Hot 100, making Grande the main craftsman to have appeared the principal single from every one of her initial four collections in the best ten of the Hot 100. In June 2018, she was included in "Bed", the second single from Nicki Minaj's fourth studio collection Queen. The subsequent single, "God Is a Woman", crested at number 8 on the Hot 100 and turned into

Grande's 10th top ten single in the US. Delivered in August 2018, Sweetener appeared at number one on the Billboard 200 and got approval from pundits. She all the while graphed nine tunes from the collection on the Hot 100, alongside cooperation, making her the fourth female craftsman to arrive at the ten-melody mark. Grande gave four shows to advance the collection, charged as The Sweetener Sessions, in New York City, Chicago, Los Angeles, and London between August 20 and September 4, 2018. In October 2018, Grande partook in the NBC broadcast, A Very Wicked Halloween, singing "The Wizard and I" from the melodic Wicked. The next month, the BBC broadcasted a one-hour exceptional, Ariana Grande the BBC, highlighting meetings and exhibitions.

In November 2018, Grande delivered the single "Express gratitude toward U, Next" and reported her fifth studio collection of a similar name. The tune appeared at number one on the Billboard Hot 100, turning into Grande's first graph beating single in the United States, burning through seven non-continuous weeks on. From that point forward, it has been guaranteed five-times platinum in the United States; the melody's music video broke records for a most-watched music video on YouTube within 24 hours of delivery and quickest Vevo video to arrive at 100 million perspectives on YouTube, the two of which were subsequently outperformed by different craftsmen. On Spotify, it turned into the quickest tune to arrive at 100 million streams (11 days) and the most-streamed tune by a female craftsman in 24 hours, with 9.6 million streams, before being outperformed by her tune "7 Rings" (almost 15 million streams). Later that very month, Grande delivered, as a team with YouTube, a four-section docuseries named Ariana Grande: Dangerous Woman Diaries. It shows in the background and show film from Grande's Dangerous Woman Tour, including minutes from the One Love Manchester show, and follows her expert life during the visit and the creation of Sweetener. The series appeared on November 29, 2018. She turned into the most streamed female craftsman of the year. In January 2019, it was reported that Grande would feature the Coachella Valley Music and Arts Festival, where she turned into the most youthful and just the fourth female craftsman ever to feature the celebration. It occurred April 12-14 and April 19-21. Grande carried a few visitor craftsmen to perform with her, including NSYNC, P. Diddy, Nicki Minaj, and Justin Bieber. Her set has gotten basic approval.

Grande's second single from Thank U, Next, "7 Rings", was delivered on January 18, 2019, and appeared at number one on the Billboard Hot 100 for the seven days of February 2, turning into her second single in succession (and generally speaking) to beat out everyone else. It made Grande the third female craftsman with numerous main introductions after Mariah Carey (3) and Britney Spears (2) and the fifth craftsman generally speaking after Justin Bieber and Drake. The tune broke a few streaming and recording industry records. Burning through eight non-sequential weeks at number one, it turned into Grande's best melody on the outline and one of the most amazing selling singles around the world. Say thanks to U, Next was delivered on February 8, 2019, and appeared at number one on the Billboard 200 while getting recognition from pundits. It broke the records for the biggest streaming week for a pop collection and a female collection in the United States with 307 million on-request streams.

Grande turned into the primary independent craftsman to possess the best three spots on the Billboard Hot 100 with "7 Rings" at number one, her third single "Say a final farewell to Your Girlfriend, I'm Bored" appearing at number two, and her lead single "Say thanks to U, Next" rose to number three, and the general second craftsman to do as such since the Beatles did in 1964 when they involved the main five spots. In the United Kingdom, Grande turned into the subsequent female independent craftsman to at the same time hold the main and two spots and the primary melodic craftsman to supplant herself at number one, two times sequentially. In February 2019, it was accounted for Grande wouldn't go to the Grammy Awards after she had a conflict with makers over an expected exhibition at the service. Grande wound up acquiring her first Grammy, for Best Pop Vocal Album, for Sweetener. That very month, Grande won a Brit Award for International

Female Solo Artist. She additionally set out on her third featuring visit, the Sweetener World Tour, to advance both Sweetener and Thank U, Next, which started on March 18, 2019. Grande was assigned for 9 honors at the 2019 Billboard Music Awards, including Top Artist. She would win two honors for Billboard Chart Achievement and Top Female Artist on May 1, 2019. Grande performed at the occasion through a pre-recorded exhibition from her Sweetener World Tour.

In June 2019, Grande reported that she co-chief delivered the soundtrack to the film Charlie's Angels; a joint effort with Miley Cyrus and Lana Del Rey, named "Don't Call Me Angel", was delivered as the lead single on September 13, 2019. It was subsequently assigned for Best Original Song, at the 24th Satellite Awards. In August 2019, she delivered a solitary named "Beau" with the pop team Social House. Grande co-composed vocalist Normani's presentation solo single "Inspiration", which was delivered on August 16, 2019. Grande won three honors at the 2019 MTV Video Music Awards, including the Artist of the Year grant. She was assigned for 12 honors altogether, including Video of the Year for "Say thanks to U, Next". Grande was highlighted on the remix of American artist and rapper Lizzo's melody "Great as Hell", which was delivered on October 25, 2019. Before the year's over, Billboard named Grande the most cultivated female craftsman to make a big appearance during the 2010s, while NME named her one of the characterizing music specialists of the ten years. She likewise turned into the most streamed female craftsman of the ten years on music web-based feature Spotify. Likewise, Forbes positioned her among the most generously compensated VIPs in 2019, sitting at number 62 on the rundown, while Billboard positioned her as 2019's most generously compensated independent artist.

POSITIONS

2020–present

In January 2020, Grande got numerous designations at the 2020 iHeartRadio Music Awards, including Female Artist of the Year. The next month, she showed up in the second period of the American TV series Kidding, which stars Jim Carrey. Grande and Justin Bieber delivered a coordinated effort tune named "Stayed with U" on May 8, 2020; net returns from the deals of the melody were given to the First Responders Children's Foundation considering the COVID-19 pandemic. The melody appeared at number one on the Billboard Hot 100, turning into Grande's third diagram beating single. Close by Bieber, the two specialists tied Mariah Carey and Drake for the most tunes to make a big appearance at number one on the Hot 100; Grande is the main craftsman to have her initial three number one's introduction at the top, following "Express gratitude toward U,

Next" and "7 Rings". Grande additionally delivered a coordinated effort with Lady Gaga, "Downpour on Me", as the second single from Gaga's 6th studio collection Chromatica. The melody additionally appeared at number one on the Billboard Hot 100, turning into Grande's fourth number-one single and assisting Grande with breaking the record for the most number-one presentations on that diagram. The tune won the Best Pop Duo/Group Performance class at the 63rd Annual Grammy Awards. In 2020, Grande turned into the most noteworthy procuring lady in music on Forbes' 2020 Celebrity 100 rundown, putting seventeenth generally speaking with $72 million. At the 2020 MTV Video Music Awards, she was named for nine honors for both "Stayed with U" (with Bieber) and "Downpour on Me" (with Gaga). For the last option, Grande accepted her third sequential assignment for Video of the Year. She won four honors, including Song of the Year for "Downpour on Me".

Grande's 6th studio collection, Positions, was delivered on October 30, 2020. It appeared at number one on the Billboard 200, turning into Grande's fifth number-one collection. The eponymous lead single was delivered on October 23. It appeared at number one on the Billboard Hot 100, turning into Grande's fifth diagram besting single and breaking various records. Grande turned into the main craftsman to have five number-one introductions on the Hot 100 and the first to have their initial five number one's presentation at the top. "Positions" turned into her third number-one single in 2020 after "Stayed with U" and "Downpour on Me", making Grande the primary craftsman since Drake to have three number-one singles in a solitary schedule year and the main female craftsman to do as such since Rihanna and Katy Perry in 2010. Close by the arrival of Positions, the melody from the collection "34+35" filled in as the subsequent single off the collection. The melody appeared at number 8, turning into Grande's eighteenth top ten single. Grande delivered a "34+35" remix including American rappers Doja Cat and Megan Thee Stallion on January 15, 2021. The remix assisted the tune with arriving at another top at number two, the most noteworthy graphing melody credited to at least three female soloists on the Hot 100 since Christina Aguilera, Mýa, Pink, and Lil' Kim's "Woman Marmalade" in 2001. The remix was one of five extra tracks remembered for the luxurious version of Positions, delivered on February 19, 2021. Grande was named the most-played craftsman on iHeartRadio's stations in 2021, coming to 2.6 billion in the crowd.

On October 14, 2020, it was declared, that Grande would star close by Leonardo DiCaprio, Jennifer Lawrence, and Meryl Streep in Don't Look Up. The film was delivered on the web-based feature Netflix, on December 24, 2021. To advance the film, Grande delivered the melody "Simply Look Up", as a team with rapper Kid Cudi, on December 3, 2021. At the 27th Critics' Choice Awards, Grande got designations in the classes Best Song and Best Acting Ensemble, as a piece of the cast. She likewise got an assignment at the 28th Screen Actors Guild Awards for Outstanding Performance by a Cast in a Motion Picture. November 13, 2020, Grande showed up on the Adult Swim Festival, performing close by music craftsman Thundercat, playing out his tune "Them Changes", which Grande had recently covered. Grande and Jennifer Hudson additionally highlighted a remix of Mariah Carey's 2010 Christmas melody "Gracious Santa!". The melody was delivered on December 4, 2020, as a feature of Mariah Carey's Magical Christmas Special. Grande delivered the show film for her Sweetener World Tour, Excuse Me, I Love You, on December 21, 2020, only on Netflix.

In March 2021, Grande had endorsed as a mentor of the twenty-first period of The Voice; Grande turned into the most generously compensated mentor in the show's set of experiences. In April, Grande highlighted on Demi Lovato's single "Met Him Last Night", and on a remix of the Weeknd's "Save Your Tears", delivered on April 23. The remix arrived at number one on the Billboard Hot 100, becoming the two craftsmen's 6th number-one single. She joined Paul McCartney as the main craftsman to acquire three number one two-part harmonies on the Hot 100. Grande and the Weeknd performed "Save Your Tears" together at the 2021 iHeartRadio Music Awards. In June, Grande included on the melody "I Don't Do Drugs" from Doja Cat's third studio collection Planet Her. Her commitment as a musician and highlighted craftsman on the tune procured Grande an assignment for Album of the Year at the 64th Annual Grammy Awards. Grande performed essentially as the feature demonstration of the "Break Tour" on the computer game Fortnite from August 6 to 8, 2021. The show pulled in 78 million players, beating Travis Scott's record of 11.7 million perspectives for his show.

In November 2021, it was declared that Grande would play Glinda for the impending movie transformation of the melodic Wicked, coordinated by Jon M. Chu and featuring close by Cynthia Erivo, who will play Elphaba.

ARTISTRY

Grande's music is for the most part pop and R&B with components of EDM, hip jump, and trap, the last option first showing up noticeably on her Christmas and Chill broadened play. While reliably keeping up with pop-R&B tones, she has expanded joining of the snare into her music as her profession has advanced on account of her work with record maker Tommy Brown. She has worked with Brown on each collection and expressed that "something I love most with regards to working with Tommy is that none of the beats he plays me at any point strong the equivalent." Grande figured out how to sound designer and produce since she adores being involved during each venture, and uncovered that Mac Miller trained her how to function with Pro Tools. Justin Tranter, a new colleague, felt motivated to perceive how elaborate Grande is in her music "from the composition to the vision to the narrating and to designing and comping her vocals." She has co-composed a few of her melodies tending to a wide assortment of subjects like love, sex, riches, separations, freedom, strengthening, self esteem, and continuing on from the past.

Grande's presentation collection, Yours Truly was commended for reproducing the R&B "energy and feel of the 90s" with the assistance of lyricist and maker Babyface. Her development, My Everything, was portrayed as an advancement from her introduction record with another sound investigating EDM and electropop classifications. She followed her pop-R&B sound on her third collection, Dangerous Woman, which was applauded by the Los Angeles Times for adjusting to various styles with the reggae-pop "Side to Side", the dance-pop-affected "Be Alright", and the combination of guitar and trap in "Once in a while". Her snare pop sound is vigorously highlighted on her fourth and fifth studio collections, Sweetener and Thank U, Next. Elias Leight of Rolling Stone accepts "with her new collection Sweetener, she put her focus on vanquishing trap, savage basslines and nervous multitudes of drum programming." She moreover "accepts the sound of tough Southern hip-bounce" investigating components of funk music with topics of affection and thriving. Craig Jenkins of Vulture composed that Grande had changed and moved toward her style to trap and hip bounce, loaded up with R&B undercurrents on Thank U, Next, with verses about separations, strengthening, and confidence. Her 6th collection, Positions, develops the R&B and trap-pop sound of Sweetener and Thank U, Next, with themes about sex and sentiment.

Grande grew up listening principally to metropolitan popular and 1990s music and says that "Over the Rainbow" was one of the main melodies she sang since "Wizard Of Oz was generally my cherished film when I was more youthful." Mariah Carey and Whitney Houston are her greatest vocal impacts: "I love Mariah Carey. She is my cherished individual in the world. Also obviously Whitney [Houston] too. To the extent vocal impacts go, Whitney and Mariah essentially cover it." Alongside Carey and Houston, Grande's other key impacts incorporate Celine Dion and Madonna. She ponders her adolescence by posting recordings of herself singing tunes from Dion's 1997 collection Let's Talk About Love on her web-based media. Grande credits Madonna for "pav[ing] the way for myself and furthermore every other female craftsman" and confessed to being "fixated on her whole discography". She acknowledged Gloria Estefan for motivating her to seek after a music profession after Estefan saw and commended Grande's exhibition on a voyage transport when she was eight years of age.

Grande commended Imogen Heap's "complicated" melody structure and named Judy Garland as a youth impact, appreciating her capacity to tell "a story when she sings". Musically, Grande appreciates India. Arie in light of the fact that her "music causes me to feel like everything will be alright" and loves Brandy's melodies since "her riffs are unquestionably right on track." Destiny's Child and Beyoncé are likewise significant impacts and motivations in her vocation. She has likewise communicated reverence for rappers who sway the music business without an arranged delivery date, telling Billboard, "My fantasy has been all of the time to be-clearly not a rapper, but rather, as, to put out music in the way that a rapper does. I feel like specific principles pop ladies are held to that men aren't. ... It's very much like, 'Broskie, I simply need to ... drop [music] the way these young men do." It roused her to deliver "Express gratitude toward U, Next" with practically no earlier declaration, which The Ringer called "all the more a Drake move as opposed to an Ariana Grande move."

Grande is a light verse soprano, having a four-octave vocal reach and a whistle register. With the arrival of Yours Truly, pundits contrasted Grande with Mariah Carey due to her wide vocal reach, sound, and melodic material. Julianne Escobedo Shepherd of Billboard composed that both Carey and Grande have "the ability to allow their vocals to communicate everything ... that is not where the similitudes end. ... Grande is undermining it with charming, agreeable, and on-pattern dresses with a ladylike inclination." Grande reacted to the correlations, "[I]t's a tremendous commendation, yet when you hear my whole collection, you'll see that Mariah's sound is very different than mine."

Steven J. Horowitz of Billboard wrote in 2014, "With her sophomore collection, the 'Issue' vocalist no longer looks like [Carey]-and that is OK."

Mark Savage of BBC News remarked, "Grande is one of pop's generally captivating and gifted artists. An attractive entertainer with unparalleled vocal control". In The New York Times, Jon Pareles composed that Grande's voice "can be sleek, hoarse or cutting, plunging through long melismas or poking out short R&B phrases; it's consistently graceful and airborne, never constrained." Composer and writer Jason Robert Brown tended to Grande in a 2016 Time magazine article: "[N]o matter the amount you are misjudged ... you will open your mouth and that mind boggling sound will come out. That remarkable, flexible, boundless instrument that permits you to close down each protest and each snag."

PUBLIC IMAGE

Grande referred to Audrey Hepburn as a significant style impact in her initial long periods of acclaim yet started to find imitating Hepburn's style "somewhat exhausting" as her profession has advanced. She likewise drew motivation from entertainers of the 1950s and 1960s, like Ann-Margret, Nancy Sinatra, and Marilyn Monroe. Grande's unassuming early examine her profession was depicted as "age-proper" in contrast with contemporary craftsmen who experienced childhood in the public eye. Jim Farber of the New York Daily News wrote in 2014 that Grande got less consideration "for how little she wears or how graphically she moves than for how she sings." That year, she deserted her previous style and started wearing short skirts and tank tops with knee-high boots in live exhibitions and honorary pathway occasions. She likewise started routinely wearing feline and rabbit ears. Lately, she started wearing curiously large coats and hoodies. Grande's style is regularly imitated by web-based media forces to be reckoned with and superstars. Following quite a while of coloring her hair red for the job of Cat Valentine, Grande wore expansions as her hair recuperated from the harm. Anne T. Donahue of MTV News noticed that her "notable" high braid has gotten more consideration than her style decisions. Even though Grande drew analysis for supposedly discourteous connections with journalists and fans in 2014, she excused the reports as "strange, incorrect portrayals". Drifter expressed: "Some might cry 'diva', but at the same time it's Grande simply standing firm to not permit others to control her picture." In July 2015, Grande started a debate in the wake of being seen on reconnaissance video in a donut shop licking doughnuts that were in plain view and saying "I disdain Americans. I disdain America. This is revolting", alluding to a plate of doughnuts. She thusly apologized, saying that she is "Amazingly glad to be an American" and that her remarks rather alluded to heftiness in the United States. She later delivered a video conciliatory sentiment for "acting inadequately". The episode was spoofed by The Muppets and highlighted in Miley Cyrus' Saturday Night Live front of "My Way", about the second thoughts of the mid-year of 2015. Grande herself made fun of the episode while facilitating Saturday Night Live in 2016, saying, "A ton of child stars wind up taking medications, or in prison, or pregnant, or get found licking a donut they didn't pay for." In 2020, she said that she quit doing interviews for some time out of dread that her words would be misinterpreted and she would be named a "diva".

Grande has an enormous after via online media. As of July 2021, her YouTube channel has more than 45 million endorsers and her music recordings have been seen an aggregate of the north of 19 billion times; her Spotify profile has amassed north of 65 million devotees, making her the second most followed craftsman and most followed female; her Instagram account has north of 255 million adherents, making her the third most followed individual and second-most followed female; her Twitter account has more than 80 million supporters, making it the seventh most-followed account; her Facebook page has north of 40 million supporters, and her TikTok has 26.3 million adherents. In May 2021, Visual Capitalist positioned Grande as the world's top female online media force to be reckoned with.

At age ten, Grande co-founded the South Florida youth singing group Kids Who Care, which performed at charitable fund-raisers and raised over $500,000 in 2007 alone. In 2009, as a member of the charitable organization Broadway in South Africa, she and her brother Frankie performed and taught music and dance to children in Gugulethu, South Africa.

She was featured with Bridgit Mendler and Kat Graham in Seventeen magazine in a 2013 public campaign to end online bullying called "Delete Digital Drama". After watching the film Blackfish that year, she urged fans to stop supporting SeaWorld. In September 2014, Grande participated at the charitable Stand Up to Cancer television program, performing her song "My Everything" in memory of her grandfather, who had died of cancer that July. Grande has adopted several rescue dogs as pets and has promoted pet adoption at her concerts. In 2016, she launched a line of lip shades, "Ariana Grande's MAC Viva Glam", with MAC Cosmetics, the profits of which benefited people affected by HIV and AIDS.

In 2015, Grande and Miley Cyrus performed a cover of Crowded House's "Don't Dream It's Over" as part of Cyrus' "Backyard Sessions" to benefit her Happy Hippie Foundation, which helps homeless and LGBT youths. Later that year, Grande headlined the Dance On the Pier event, part of the LGBT Pride Week in New York City. As a feminist, Grande wrote a well-received, "empowering" essay on Twitter decrying the double standard and misogyny in the focus of the press on female musicians' relationships and sex lives instead of "their value as an individual". She noted that she has "more to talk about" concerning her music and accomplishments rather than her romantic relationships. In 2016, E! writer Kendall Fisher called her "a feminist hero". That year, Grande joined Madonna to raise funds for orphaned children in Malawi; she and Victoria Monét recorded "Better Days" in support of the

Black Lives Matter movement. To aid the victims of the Manchester Arena bombing in 2017, Grande organized the One Love Manchester concert and re-released "One Last Time" and her live performance of "Over the Rainbow" at the event as charity singles. The total amount raised was reported $23 million (more than £17 million), and she received praise for her "grace and strength" in leading the benefit concert. Madeline Roth of MTV wrote that the performance "bolstered courage among an audience that desperately needed it. ... Returning to the stage was a true act of bravery and resilience". In 2017, New York magazine's Vulture section ranked the event as the No. 1 concert of the year, and Billboard's Mitchell Harrison called Grande a "gay icon" for her LGBT-friendly lyrics and performances and "support for the LGBTQ community".

In September 2017, Grande performed in A Concert for Charlottesville which benefitted the victims of the August 2017 white nationalist rally in Charlottesville, Virginia. In March 2018, she participated in March for Our Lives to support gun control reform. Grande donated the proceeds from the first show in Atlanta on her Sweetener World Tour to Planned Parenthood in a response to the passage of several anti-abortion laws in several states including Georgia. During the COVID-19 pandemic, Grande donated between $500 and $1,000 each to several fans as financial support. Grande also supported a COVID-19 fund named Project 100, which aimed to provide $1,000 digital payments to 100,000 families who have been greatly impacted by the pandemic. In May 2020, Grande announced that all net proceeds from her collaboration with singer Justin Bieber, "Stuck With U", would be donated to the First Responders Children's Foundation to fund grants and scholarships for children of frontline workers who are working during the global pandemic. That month, Grande joined a Los Angeles protest against the murder of George Floyd, demanding justice and asking fans to sign petitions condemning the act of police brutality. She highlighted white privilege and called for more activism outside social media. In December 2020, Grande, Scott, Brian Nicholson, her choreographers, and friends launched "Orange Twins Rescue", an animal rescue center based in Los Angeles. In the same month, Grande surprised kids, who spend the holiday at children's hospitals in L.A. and the UK, with gifts from wish lists at the UCLA Mattel Children's Hospital and the Royal Manchester Children's Hospital.

In June 2021, Grande, along with a dozen other celebrities signed an open letter to Congress to pass the Equality Act highlighting the Act would protect "marginalized communities". In the same month, Grande partnered with the online portal BetterHelp and gave away $2 million worth of therapy to fans.

In October 2014, Grande joined the bottled water brand WAT-AAH! as an equity holder and partner. In November 2015, she released a limited-edition handbag in collaboration with Coach. In January

2016, she launched a makeup collection with MAC Cosmetics, donating 100% of proceeds to the MAC AIDS Fund. In February 2016, Grande launched a fashion line with Lipsy London. Later that year, she teamed up with Brookstone, using the concept art of artist Wenqing Yan, to design cat ear headphones. In 2017, Grande collaborated with Square Enix to create a character based on herself for the mobile game Final Fantasy Brave Exvius. Grande was a limited-time unlockable character as part of the Dangerous Woman Tour event, which also included an orchestral remix of Grande's song "Touch It"; the character, Dangerous Ariana, is a magical support character who uses music-based attacks. In September 2017, she became a brand ambassador for Reebok. In August 2018, she partnered with American Express for The Sweetener Sessions, a partnership that continued through the Sweetener World Tour in 2019, alongside T-Mobile. In March 2019, she partnered with Starbucks for the launch of the Cloud Macchiato beverage. In May 2019, Grande was announced as the face of Givenchy's Fall-Winter campaign. The campaign began in July and generated $25.13 million in media impact value. Beats, Samsung, Fiat, Reebok, and Guess products have been featured in Grande's music videos. She has appeared in commercials for Macy's, T-Mobile, and Apple, as well as for her fragrances.

Grande has released eight fragrances with Luxe Brands. She launched her debut fragrance, Ari by Ariana Grande, in 2015. In the wake of its success, she launched her second fragrance, Sweet Like Candy, in 2016. Her third fragrance, Moonlight, was released in 2017; her latest fragrances, Cloud, Thank U, Next, R.E.M., God Is A Woman, launched in 2018, 2019, and 2020, respectively. The collection also included the limited editions Frankie (2016), Sweet Like Candy Limited Edition (2017), Thank U, Next 2.0, and Cloud Intense (2021). The fragrances won the Fragrance Foundation Award multiple times, most recently with R.E.M. in 2021. Since its launch in 2015, the franchise has made $750 million in retail sales globally. In November 2021, Grande launched her makeup line, "R.E.M. Beauty".

PERSONAL LIFE

Grande has said she battled with hypoglycemia, which she ascribed to helpless dietary propensities. She likewise experienced post-awful pressure issues (PTSD) and tension after the Manchester Arena bombarding; she almost pulled out of her presentation in the 2018 transmission A Very Wicked Halloween because of uneasiness. Grande has additionally said she has been getting help for north of 10 years, having first seen emotional wellness proficient soon after her folks' separation.

Grande was raised Roman Catholic however deserted the congregation during the pontificate of Benedict XVI, contradicting its position on homosexuality and noticing that her relative Frankie is gay. She and Frankie have followed the lessons of Kabbalah, a part of Jewish magic since she was 12. She said that they accept "the premise lies in the possibility that assuming you're benevolent to other people, beneficial things will happen to you". A few of her tunes, for example, "Make You extremely upset Right Back", are steady of LGBT freedoms. She has likewise been marked "a promoter for a sex-uplifting outlook".

In November 2019, Grande embraced Senator Bernie Sanders' second official bid.

Grande met entertainer Graham Phillips in the cast of the Broadway melodic 13 of every 2008 and dated him until 2011. From October 2014 to April 2015, she dated rapper.

In the wake of recording "The Way" with Mac Miller in 2012, the two started dating in 2016. They worked together on the single "My Favorite Part", delivered in September 2016 on Miller's collection The Divine Feminine (2016). Their relationship finished in May 2018. That September, Miller passed on from an inadvertent medication glut; Grande communicated despondency over his demise via web-based media and referred to him her as "closest companion."

In May 2018, Grande started dating entertainer and jokester Pete Davidson, and they became connected the following month. They canceled their commitment and cut off the friendship in October 2018.

Grande started dating realtor Dalton Gomez in January 2020. Their relationship, while generally private, was unveiled in the music video of her and Justin Bieber's good cause single "Stayed With U". Grande reported their commitment on December

20, 2020, following 11 months of dating. On May 15, 2021, they wedded in a private service at her home in Montecito, California, where she wore a custom Vera Wang dress. Her wedding pictures turned into the most-enjoyed Instagram post by a VIP, with more than 25 million preferences.

ACHIEVEMENTS

Each of Grande's full-length collections have been affirmed platinum or higher by the RIAA. Having amassed 90 billion streams up to this point, Grande is the most streamed female craftsman ever; she is additionally the most streamed female craftsman on Spotify and Apple Music. Grande has won two Grammy Awards, one BRIT Award, nine MTV Video Music Awards, three MTV Europe Music Awards, and three American Music Awards. She has gotten 22 Billboard Music Award designations and won two out of 2019, including Top Female Artist. Grande has won eight Nickelodeon Kids' Choice Awards, remembering one for 2014 for Favorite TV Actress for her exhibition on Sam and Cat, and three People's Choice Awards. In 2014, she got the Breakthrough Artist of the Year Award from the Music Business Association and Best Newcomer at the Bambi Awards. She has won six iHeartRadio Music Awards and twelve Teen Choice Awards. She was named Billboard Women in Music's Rising Star in 2014 and Woman of the Year in 2018. Starting at 2021, Grande has broken north of twenty Guinness World Records by accomplishing "most tunes to make a big appearance at number one on the Billboard Hot 100" with five tunes at the highest rated spot. Across collections, singles, and elements (when physical, downloads, and streaming identical deals are joined), Grande has been ensured for 85.5 million units in the U.S, and she is the fifth-most elevated affirmed female computerized singles craftsman, with 63 million absolute units guaranteed by the Recording Industry Association of America (RIAA). Grande is likewise guaranteed for 20.4 million units in the UK.

Grande has broken various Hot 100 records. Grande has an aggregate of sixteen top ten makes a big appearance hitherto, starting with her first single "The Way"; the lead single from every one of her initial five studio collections has appeared in the main ten, making her the main craftsman to accomplish this. In 2020, she turned into the primary demonstration to have her initial five number-one singles, "Express gratitude toward U, Next", "7 Rings", "Stayed With U", "Downpour on Me", and "Positions" debut at number one; that year, Grande likewise broke the record for the most number-one introductions. Grande would likewise turn into the primary craftsman to have three singles debut at number one on a solitary schedule year. She later broke the record for most at the same time graphing tunes on the main 40 of the Hot 100 for a female craftsman with the arrival of her fifth studio collection, Thank U, Next, when eleven of the twelve tracks outlined inside the district (later outperformed by Billie Eilish). The three singles from Thank U, Next, "7 Rings", "Part ways with Your Girlfriend, I'm Bored", and "Say thanks to U, Next" diagrammed at numbers one, two, and three individually on the seven day stretch of February 23, 2019, making Grande the primary independent craftsman to involve the best three spots of the Billboard Hot 100 and the principal craftsman to do as such since the Beatles in 1964. With her collection Thank U, Next, Grande set the standard for the biggest streaming week for a pop collection and a female craftsman, with 307 million on-request sound streams. As of May 2021, Grande has 71 passages on the Hot 100, turning into the fourth female craftsman with the most Hot 100 sections.

In 2016 and 2019, Grande was named one of Time's 100 most compelling individuals on the planet. In 2017, Celia Almeida composed an article for Miami New Times and accepts that of the relative multitude of greatest pop stars of the beyond 20 years, Grande has made the most persuading progress "from ingénue to an autonomous female craftsman." In 2020, Bloomberg named Grande the "primary pop diva of the streaming age". Grande was additionally positioned on Pitchfork's rundown of "The 200 Most Important Artists of Pitchfork's First 25 Years", expressing, "after a time of awful misfortune, Grande withdrew and reset, in the end arising with music that drove her masterfulness further as it attested an otherworldly trifecta of trust, euphoria, and a stalwart voice". "Say thanks to U, Next" was remembered for Rolling Stone's 2021 update of their 500 Greatest Songs of All Time. In 2021, Grande positioned 78th on Billboard's Greatest of All Time Hot 100 Artists.

THANK YOU

Manufactured by Amazon.ca
Bolton, ON